# 300 Trashy Truths You Didn't Need to Know

## Your Great Big Grab Bag of Useless Helpful Tidbits

Michael Clutton

Published by Michael Clutton, 2024.

300 TRASHY TRUTHS YOU DIDN'T NEED TO KNOW

**First edition. July 2, 2024.**



ISBN: 979-8227689917

Written by Michael Clutton.

# Table of Contents

# Introduction

Whether you're a seasoned recycler, an eco-curious skeptic, or someone who loves quirky facts, this booklet is your perfect companion for navigating the fascinating, often perplexing world of recycling.

Recycling, a seemingly simple act of tossing a plastic bottle into a designated bin, is far more complex and layered than it appears. This booklet aims to unravel the mysteries, debunk the myths, and reveal the surprising truths behind this global practice. From the ancient origins of recycling to the modern-day economic and political landscapes, we will dive deep into the nuances of recycling, exploring its impacts, benefits, and, sometimes, its inefficiencies.

What's the point? Well, if you've ever wondered what happens to your recyclables after they leave the curbside, if you're curious about the actual environmental impact of recycling, or if you enjoy fun and obscure trivia, then this book is for you. We promise a mix of practical information and entertaining tidbits to educate and amuse.

So, fasten your seatbelt and prepare for an enlightening journey through the world of recycling. Let's sort through the facts and fiction together and uncover your recycling bin's hidden gems and surprising truths.

# Chapter 1: The Origins of Recycling

Recycling is often thought of as a modern innovation, but its roots can be traced back thousands of years. Ancient civilizations understood the value of reusing materials long before it became a global movement.

## Early Recycling Practices in Ancient Civilizations

In 1031, Japan set a precedent by recycling paper. Discarded documents and letters were repulped into new sheets, showcasing an early form of resource conservation. Similarly, in ancient Rome, bronze coins were melted down and recast to meet the constant demand for currency. This practice conserved precious metals and reflected a practical approach to resource management.

Glass recycling was common in Europe during the medieval period. Broken glass was collected and melted to create new glassware, a practice that persisted well into the Renaissance. This early form of recycling was driven by necessity rather than environmental consciousness, as materials were often scarce and expensive.

## The Rise of Modern Recycling in the 1960s and 1970s

The modern recycling movement gained momentum in the late 1960s and early 1970s. The environmental movement, spurred by growing awareness of pollution and resource depletion, played a crucial role. Earth Day, first celebrated in 1970, marked a significant milestone in raising public consciousness about environmental issues, including the importance of recycling.

The recycling symbol, now ubiquitous, was designed by Gary Anderson, a 23-year-old engineering student, in 1970 as part of a contest. His design, three chasing arrows forming a triangle, became an enduring icon of the recycling movement.

Municipal recycling programs began to appear in the 1970s, with University City, Missouri, pioneering the first curbside collection program in 1973. These early initiatives laid the foundation for the widespread adoption of today's recycling practices.

**Key Figures and Campaigns That Popularized Recycling**

Several vital figures and campaigns have been instrumental in popularizing recycling. Barry Commoner, an American biologist, and Paul Connett, an environmental chemist, were vocal advocates for waste management and recycling. Their efforts, grassroots campaigns, and community activism helped shift public perception and policy toward sustainable practices.

The "Reduce, Reuse, Recycle" campaign, introduced in the 1970s, encapsulated the core principles of waste reduction and resource conservation. This catchy slogan, educational programs, and media campaigns played a pivotal role in embedding recycling into everyday life.

**Grab Bag of Useless Helpful Tidbits on Recycling Origins**

**Useless Helpful Tidbit 1:** In ancient Athens, the government banned the disposal of olive oil jars to encourage their reuse, an early example of a recycling policy.

**Useless Helpful Tidbit 2:** During World War II, Britain ran a massive campaign to recycle scrap metal for use in weapons and vehicles, famously collecting iron railings and pots.

**Useless Helpful Tidbit 3:** Ancient Chinese cities had designated areas for recycling organic waste into fertilizer, demonstrating early sustainable agriculture practices.

**Useless Helpful Tidbit 4:** The first known use of recycled glass dates back to 2000 BC in Mesopotamia, where glass fragments were melted and reshaped.

**Useless Helpful Tidbit 5:** Medieval blacksmiths often recycled iron and steel from old tools and weapons to create new ones, a practice that conserved valuable resources.

**Useless Helpful Tidbit 6:** In 1776, the U.S. Continental Congress encouraged citizens to recycle old metal items to support the Revolutionary War effort.

**Useless Helpful Tidbit 7:** By the 19th century, Paris had a thriving recycling market for old clothes and rags used to make paper.

**Useless Helpful Tidbit 8:** The Japanese "Mottainai" philosophy, which emphasizes waste minimization and reuse, dates back centuries and has influenced modern recycling practices in Japan.

**Useless Helpful Tidbit 9:** In the early 1900s, New York City's sanitation department implemented a waste separation system that included recycling paper, metals, and glass.

**Useless Helpful Tidbit 10:** During the Victorian era, London's "rag-and-bone" men collected unwanted household items sold to merchants for recycling and repurposing.

**Useless Helpful Tidbit 11:** The first recorded instance of aluminum can recycling took place in 1904 when a facility in Chicago began to process used cans.

**Useless Helpful Tidbit 12:** In the 19th century, Parisian "rag pickers" were a common sight. These individuals collected discarded textiles, bones, and other materials for resale and recycling.

**Useless Helpful Tidbit 13:** During the American Civil War, the Union and Confederate armies recycled spent bullets and cannonballs to make new ammunition.

**Useless Helpful Tidbit 14:** The concept of "zero waste," which emphasizes reusing and recycling everything, has its roots in the Japanese Edo period, where almost every material was repurposed.

**Useless Helpful Tidbit 15:** In 1940s Britain, recycling was promoted as a patriotic duty to support the war effort, leading to the widespread collection of metal, rubber, and paper.

**Useless Helpful Tidbit 16:** The ancient Mayans practiced recycling by using broken pottery shards to construct and repair their buildings.

**Useless Helpful Tidbit 17:** New York City introduced its first recycling plant in 1897, processing rags, newspapers, and dead horses.

**Useless Helpful Tidbit 18:** In ancient Greece, broken pottery was often used as a cheap material for making roads and paths, a form of early recycling.

**Useless Helpful Tidbit 19:** In medieval England, animal bones were collected and used to create buttons, combs, and other household items, showcasing the early recycling of organic materials.

**Useless Helpful Tidbit 20:** In 2003, San Francisco implemented a mandatory composting program, one of the first of its kind in the United States, significantly reducing landfill waste.

**Great Big Grab Bag of Fun Factoids**

**Fun Factoid 1:** Recycling one ton of paper saves about 17 trees, 380 gallons of oil, and 7,000 gallons of water.

**Fun Factoid 2:** The energy saved by recycling one glass bottle can power a light bulb for four hours.

**Fun Factoid 3:** Thanks to recycling, approximately 75% of the aluminum ever produced is still in use today.

**Fun Factoid 4:** The recycling industry in the United States is worth $236 billion a year and provides more than 500,000 jobs.

**Fun Factoid 5:** In 2018, China, once the world's largest importer of recyclables, banned the import of certain types of waste, causing a global shift in recycling practices.

# Chapter 2: Myths vs. Facts

Recycling is a noble endeavor, but it's also shrouded in myths and misconceptions. Understanding the truths behind these myths can help us become more effective recyclers and make more informed choices. Let's delve into some of the most common misconceptions about recycling and uncover the facts that set them straight.

**Common Misconceptions About Recycling**

One prevalent myth is that all plastics are recyclable. In reality, not all plastics can be processed by recycling facilities. Plastics are categorized into different types based on their chemical composition, and only certain types, like PET (Polyethylene Terephthalate) and HDPE (High-Density Polyethylene), are widely accepted for recycling.

Another common misconception is that biodegradable plastics are an eco-friendly alternative to regular plastics. While they break down faster than traditional plastics, they often require specific conditions, such as high temperatures in industrial composting facilities. They can also leave behind microplastics, which can harm the environment.

Myths also surround glass recycling. Many people believe that all glass can be recycled indefinitely. While it's true that glass can be recycled multiple times without losing quality, colored glass (like green and brown) is often less desirable because it can contaminate clear glass streams and is more challenging to recycle into new products.

**Debunking Myths with Factual Information**

Let's tackle the myth that recycling uses more energy than it saves. This is a persistent misconception. Recycling aluminum, for example, uses about 95% less energy than producing new aluminum from raw materials. Similarly, recycling paper saves approximately 60% of the energy compared to making new paper from virgin pulp.

Another myth is that rinsing recyclables wastes water and negates the benefits of recycling. While cleaning out food residues to avoid contamination is essential, you don't need to use copious amounts of water. A quick rinse or wiping with a used napkin is usually sufficient.

Then, there's the belief that one contaminated item can ruin an entire batch of recyclables. While contamination is a severe issue, recycling facilities are equipped to handle a certain level of contamination. However, it's always best to follow local guidelines to minimize the impact.

**Grab Bag of Useless Helpful Tidbits on Recycling Myths**

**Useless Helpful Tidbit 1:** Myth: Recyclable items can be placed in plastic bags. Fact: Plastic bags can jam sorting machines, and recyclables should be discarded in bins.

**Useless Helpful Tidbit 2:** Myth: All electronic devices are easily recyclable. Fact: Electronics contain hazardous materials and require specialized recycling processes.

**Useless Helpful Tidbit 3:** Myth: Food containers must be spotless to be recycled. Fact: A little residue is acceptable; thorough rinsing is not necessary.

**Useless Helpful Tidbit 4:** Myth: Recycling is only for environmentalists. Fact: Recycling has economic benefits, including job creation and resource conservation.

**Useless Helpful Tidbit 5:** Myth: Compostable plastics can be recycled with regular plastics. Fact: Compostable plastics contaminate plastic recycling streams and should be composted.

**Useless Helpful Tidbit 6:** Myth: Bottle caps must be removed before recycling. Fact: Most recycling programs now accept caps if they are screwed back on the empty bottle.

**Useless Helpful Tidbit 7:** Myth: Recycling paper removes the need for virgin pulp. Fact: Paper fibers shorten each time they are recycled, eventually requiring new pulp.

**Useless Helpful Tidbit 8:** Myth: Glass recycling saves more energy than it uses. Fact: While glass recycling is beneficial, the energy savings vary depending on transportation and processing.

**Useless Helpful Tidbit 9:** Myth: Shredded paper is easily recyclable. Fact: Shredded paper can clog machinery and is often unacceptable in curbside recycling.

**Useless Helpful Tidbit 10:** Myth: All cardboard is recyclable. Fact: Wax-coated or greasy cardboard, like pizza boxes, can contaminate the recycling stream.

**Useless Helpful Tidbit 11:** Myth: Only large items are worth recycling. Fact: Small items, like bottle caps and aluminum foil, can be recycled and have significant impacts.

**Useless Helpful Tidbit 12:** Myth: Items with recycling symbols are always recyclable. Fact: The symbol indicates the type of material, not whether it can be recycled in your area.

**Useless Helpful Tidbit 13:** Myth: Used paper towels and napkins can be recycled. Fact: These items are often contaminated with food waste and are not recyclable.

**Useless Helpful Tidbit 14:** Myth: Recycling is the same everywhere. Fact: Recycling rules and capabilities vary widely by location.

**Useless Helpful Tidbit 15:** Myth: Incandescent light bulbs can be recycled curbside. Fact: These bulbs contain materials that require special handling and are not accepted in curbside programs.

**Useless Helpful Tidbit 16:** Myth: Old clothes can go in the recycling bin. Fact: Textiles require separate recycling processes and should be taken to specialized facilities.

**Useless Helpful Tidbit 17:** Myth: Metal lids can't be recycled with glass jars. Fact: Metal lids can often be recycled separately from glass containers.

**Useless Helpful Tidbit 18:** Myth: Biodegradable items can go in the recycling bin. Fact: Biodegradable items need composting conditions to break down properly.

**Useless Helpful Tidbit 19:** Myth: All recycling is processed domestically. Fact: Many countries export recyclables to other nations for processing.

**Useless Helpful Tidbit 20:** Myth: Recycled materials are of lower quality. Fact: Many recycled materials are of high quality and meet industry standards.

## Great Big Grab Bag of Fun Factoids

**Fun Factoid 1:** In San Francisco, a city ordinance mandates recycling and composting, leading to a waste diversion rate of over 80%.

**Fun Factoid 2:** Recycling one ton of aluminum cans conserves more than five metric tons of $CO_2$ emissions.

**Fun Factoid 3:** The EPA estimates that recycling and composting in the U.S. prevented about 186 million metric tons of $CO_2$ emissions in 2018.

**Fun Factoid 4:** The recycling rate for lead-acid batteries in the U.S. is nearly 99%, making them the most recycled consumer product.

**Fun Factoid 5:** Switzerland has one of the highest recycling rates in the world, with about 52% of municipal waste being recycled.

# Chapter 3: The Economics of Recycling

Recycling isn't just an environmental issue—it's also a significant economic one. The costs involved in promoting and facilitating recycling programs and the economic benefits and savings they provide can vary widely depending on the region. By understanding these financial aspects, we can better appreciate the complex balance between the cost and benefit of recycling.

**Costs Involved in Promoting and Facilitating Recycling**

Promoting and facilitating recycling programs can be costly. Municipalities often bear the brunt of these expenses, covering costs related to collection, sorting, and processing recyclables. Investment in recycling infrastructure—such as bins, trucks, and sorting facilities—can require substantial upfront capital. Public education campaigns to encourage recycling participation also add to the costs.

However, these expenses can be offset by various savings and revenue streams. For example, recycling reduces the need for landfill space, which can be costly to maintain and expand. Furthermore, the sale of recycled materials can generate revenue, helping to subsidize the costs of the programs.

**Economic Benefits and Savings from Recycling Programs**

Recycling programs offer significant economic benefits. They create jobs across the recycling chain, from collection and sorting to processing and selling recycled materials. These jobs often provide stable employment opportunities in communities, contributing to local economies.

Moreover, recycling conserves natural resources and reduces energy consumption, lowering production costs for manufacturers who use recycled materials. For instance, producing aluminum from recycled cans uses 95% less energy than raw materials. This energy savings translates into cost savings for manufacturers and consumers.

**Comparison of Expenses and Savings in Different Regions**

The financial dynamics of recycling can differ dramatically from one region to another. In some areas, strong markets for recycled materials and efficient recycling systems make recycling economically viable and profitable. In other places, the lack of infrastructure and markets can burden recycling financially.

For example, in countries like Germany and Sweden, advanced recycling systems and high participation rates make recycling programs highly efficient and cost-effective. In contrast, in many developing countries, the lack of infrastructure and public awareness can make recycling programs challenging to implement and sustain financially.

**Grab a Bag of Useless, Helpful Tidbits on the Financial Aspects of Recycling**

**Useless Helpful Tidbit 1:** The cost of recycling a ton of plastic ranges from $200 to $400, while the revenue generated from selling recycled plastic can be as high as $600 per ton.

**Useless Helpful Tidbit 2:** Recycling one ton of aluminum can generate revenue of over $1,000, significantly higher than the cost of recycling, which is about $200 per ton.

**Useless Helpful Tidbit 3:** New York City spends approximately $300 million annually on its recycling program but saves around $20 million in landfill costs each year.

**Useless Helpful Tidbit 4:** In 2018, the U.S. recycling industry generated nearly $110 billion in economic activity and provided over 500,000 jobs.

**Useless Helpful Tidbit 5:** The European Union's recycling industry is valued at approximately €24 billion, highlighting its economic significance in Europe.

**Useless Helpful Tidbit 6:** Implementing a recycling program in a city with a population of 100,000 can cost between $500,000 and $1 million per year but generate significant savings and revenue.

**Useless Helpful Tidbit 7:** In Japan, the cost of recycling is partially offset by a system of eco-taxes on products, which funds recycling programs and encourages manufacturers to design recyclable products.

**Useless Helpful Tidbit 8:** Recycling one ton of paper saves approximately $50 in landfill costs, contributing to overall municipal savings.

**Useless Helpful Tidbit 9:** In the UK, the recycling industry supports over 70,000 jobs and contributes around £6.8 billion annually to the economy.

**Useless Helpful Tidbit 10:** In San Francisco, the mandatory recycling and composting ordinance saves the city an estimated $25 million annually in landfill costs.

**Useless Helpful Tidbit 11:** The energy savings from recycling one ton of glass is equivalent to the amount of energy a typical household uses for over a month.

**Useless Helpful Tidbit 12:** South Korea's aggressive recycling policies have reduced waste disposal costs by about $10 million annually.

**Useless Helpful Tidbit 13:** Germany's recycling system, known as the Green Dot program, is financed by packaging manufacturers and has significantly reduced municipal waste management costs.

**Useless Helpful Tidbit 14:** In Australia, recycling one ton of steel can save the equivalent of 2,500 kilowatt-hours of electricity, reducing costs and environmental impact.

**Useless Helpful Tidbit 15:** The global market for recycled metals is valued at over $300 billion, with significant contributions from aluminum, copper, and steel recycling.

**Useless Helpful Tidbit 16:** In Canada, the Blue Box recycling program generates approximately $1.6 billion in economic activity annually.

**Useless Helpful Tidbit 17:** Recycling rates in Norway are among the highest in the world, with nearly 97% of plastic bottles being recycled, saving substantial municipal costs.

**Useless Helpful Tidbit 18:** Singapore's waste management system, which includes extensive recycling, saves the city-state around $50 million annually in waste disposal costs.

**Useless Helpful Tidbit 19:** In Brazil, the recycling of aluminum cans is so efficient that the country recycles over 98% of its aluminum, generating significant economic returns.

**Useless Helpful Tidbit 20:** The U.S. landfill disposal cost averages around $55 per ton, making recycling a financially attractive alternative for many municipalities.

**Great Big Grab Bag of Fun Factoids**
**Fun Factoid 1:** The global recycling industry is valued at over $500 billion, reflecting its immense economic importance.

**Fun Factoid 2:** Recycling one ton of steel conserves 2,500 pounds of iron ore, 1,400 pounds of coal, and 120 pounds of limestone, reducing production costs and environmental impact.

**Fun Factoid 3:** 2017 China processed about 45% of the world's plastic waste imports, generating substantial revenue before implementing strict import bans in 2018.

**Fun Factoid 4:** Implementing pay-as-you-throw programs, where residents are charged based on the amount of waste they produce, has increased recycling rates and reduced waste management costs in many U.S. cities.

**Fun Factoid 5:** The U.S. recycling industry supports more jobs than the U.S. auto industry, highlighting its significant economic role.

# Chapter 4: The Politics Behind Recycling

Government regulations, lobbying, and corporate interests heavily influence recycling policies and practices. Understanding these political dynamics is crucial for understanding the complexities of recycling programs and their varied success across regions.

**Government Policies and Regulations**

Government policies play a pivotal role in shaping recycling practices. Regulations determine what materials can be recycled, how they should be processed, and the incentives for recycling. For instance, extended producer responsibility (EPR) laws require manufacturers to manage the disposal of their products, encouraging eco-friendly designs and increased recycling rates. Policies like these can drive significant improvements in recycling efficiency and effectiveness.

**Influence of Lobbying and Corporate Interests**

Lobbying and corporate interests also exert substantial influence over recycling policies. Industry groups often lobby for regulations that favor their economic interests, which can sometimes undermine environmental goals. For example, the plastic industry has historically lobbied against stricter recycling mandates and supported less stringent regulations that allow for more excellent production and use of single-use plastics.

**Case Studies of Successful and Failed Recycling Programs**

Examining case studies of both successful and failed recycling programs provides valuable insights into what works and what doesn't. Countries like Germany and Sweden boast highly efficient recycling systems due to comprehensive regulations, strong public participation, and advanced infrastructure. In contrast, other regions struggle with ineffective programs due to insufficient infrastructure, insufficient funding, or weak regulatory frameworks. These case studies highlight the importance of cohesive policies, public engagement, and proper funding.

**Grab a Bag of Useless, Helpful Tidbits on the Political Landscape of Recycling**

**Useless Helpful Tidbit 1:** The EU's Waste Framework Directive mandates that all member states recycle at least 50% of household waste by 2020.

**Useless Helpful Tidbit 2:** California's Bottle Bill, enacted in 1987, incentivizes recycling by providing a refund value for beverage containers.

**Useless Helpful Tidbit 3:** Germany's Packaging Act requires producers to contribute to the costs of collecting and recycling packaging waste.

**Useless Helpful Tidbit 4:** The Basel Convention, an international treaty, controls the transboundary movements of hazardous wastes and their disposal.

**Useless Helpful Tidbit 5:** In 2019, China implemented its National Sword policy, banning the import of most plastics and other materials to improve domestic recycling.

**Useless Helpful Tidbit 6:** The U.S. has no federal recycling law, so states and municipalities are left to develop their own regulations and programs.

**Useless Helpful Tidbit 7:** Extended Producer Responsibility (EPR) laws in Japan require manufacturers to take back and recycle electronic waste.

**Useless Helpful Tidbit 8:** The Ocean Conservancy's Trash Free Seas Alliance works with governments and corporations to reduce marine debris through better waste management policies.

**Useless Helpful Tidbit 9:** The influence of the American Chemistry Council has led to significant lobbying efforts against plastic bag bans in various states.

**Useless Helpful Tidbit 10:** Sweden charges households a fee for waste collection that decreases as the amount of waste they produce goes down, encouraging recycling.

**Useless Helpful Tidbit 11:** Norway's deposit return scheme for beverage containers has achieved a return rate of over 97%.

**Useless Helpful Tidbit 12:** The European Green Deal includes a Circular Economy Action Plan to make sustainable products the norm in the EU.

**Useless Helpful Tidbit 13:** The Indian government's Plastic Waste Management Rules require the phasing out non-recyclable and multi-layered plastic packaging.

**Useless Helpful Tidbit 14:** In Canada, the province of British Columbia has implemented an EPR program that covers over 77% of the population.

**Useless Helpful Tidbit 15:** In the UK, the Environment Act 2021 includes measures to increase recycling rates and reduce waste, such as introducing a deposit return scheme.

**Useless Helpful Tidbit 16:** Ireland's plastic bag levy, introduced in 2002, reduced plastic bag use by 90% within the first year.

**Useless Helpful Tidbit 17:** South Korea's Volume-based Waste Fee system charges residents based on how much they discard, promoting recycling and waste reduction.

**Useless Helpful Tidbit 18:** The Alliance to End Plastic Waste, consisting of major global corporations, aims to invest $1.5 billion in solutions to eliminate plastic waste in the environment.

**Useless Helpful Tidbit 19:** In the Netherlands, the government has set a target to recycle 65% of municipal waste by 2025.

**Useless Helpful Tidbit 20:** The UN Environment Programme's Clean Seas campaign has garnered commitments from over 60 countries to reduce plastic waste through improved policies.

**Great Big Grab Bag of Fun Factoids**

**Fun Factoid 1:** The German Green Dot system, introduced in 1991, was the first national packaging recycling scheme and has since been adopted by over 30 countries.

**Fun Factoid 2:** In 2017, New York City passed the Zero Waste Act, aiming to eliminate waste from landfills by 2030 through increased recycling and composting efforts.

**Fun Factoid 3:** The Norwegian recycling system is so efficient that it imports waste from other countries to keep its recycling plants running.

**Fun Factoid 4:** Rwanda has one of the strictest plastic bag bans in the world, implemented in 2008, and has since maintained a largely plastic-free environment.

**Fun Factoid 5:** The EU Waste Electrical and Electronic Equipment (WEEE) Directive aims to reduce the environmental impact of e-waste by setting collection, recycling, and recovery targets for electronic goods.

# Chapter 5: Global Impact of Recycling

Recycling is crucial in mitigating environmental degradation, conserving resources, and reducing waste. Its impact is felt globally through international efforts and agreements that aim to standardize practices and improve outcomes. By examining the environmental and ecological effects of recycling, we can better understand its significance in preserving our planet.

**How Recycling Affects the Environment and Ecosystems**

Recycling reduces the need for raw material extraction, often involving destructive processes such as mining and deforestation. This helps preserve natural habitats and biodiversity. Additionally, recycling lowers greenhouse gas emissions by saving energy in manufacturing processes. For example, producing aluminum from recycled materials uses 95% less energy than making it from raw bauxite ore.

**International Recycling Efforts and Agreements**

International agreements and efforts, such as the Basel Convention and the European Union's Circular Economy Action Plan, aim to regulate and enhance recycling practices globally. These initiatives encourage countries to adopt standardized recycling protocols, reduce waste exports, and invest in domestic recycling infrastructure. Collaborative efforts like these are essential in addressing the global waste crisis and promoting sustainable resource management.

**The Impact of Recycling on Reducing Waste and Conserving Resources**

Recycling significantly reduces the volume of waste sent to landfills and incinerators, conserving space and reducing pollution. It also conserves natural resources by reusing materials that would otherwise require new extraction. For example, recycling one ton of paper saves 17 trees and 7,000 gallons of water. These resource savings highlight the importance of recycling in sustainable development.

**Grab a Bag of Useless, Helpful Tidbits on the Global Impact of Recycling**

**Useless Helpful Tidbit 1:** Germany's recycling rate is over 65%, one of the highest in the world, thanks to comprehensive recycling policies and public participation.

**Useless Helpful Tidbit 2:** Recycling aluminum saves 95% of the energy required to make the same amount from virgin sources, significantly reducing greenhouse gas emissions.

**Useless Helpful Tidbit 3:** Japan recycles approximately 77% of its plastic waste, making it a global leader in plastic recycling efforts.

**Useless Helpful Tidbit 4:** The European Union's Circular Economy Action Plan aims to make sustainable products the norm by 2030, promoting recycling and reducing waste.

**Useless Helpful Tidbit 5:** Recycling one ton of paper can save about 17 trees, 380 gallons of oil, and 4,000 kilowatts of energy.

**Useless Helpful Tidbit 6:** Sweden's waste management system recycles or composts 99% of household waste, with only 1% going to landfills.

**Useless Helpful Tidbit 7:** The recycling industry in the United States creates approximately 757,000 jobs and generates $36.6 billion in wages annually.

**Useless Helpful Tidbit 8:** In 2020, the global recycling rate for PET plastic bottles was 56%, with Europe achieving the highest rate at 74%.

**Useless Helpful Tidbit 9:** Recycling steel saves 74% of the energy needed to produce it from raw materials, contributing to significant energy conservation.

**Useless Helpful Tidbit 10:** San Francisco aims to achieve zero waste by 2030, diverting 80% of its waste from landfills through recycling and composting.

**Useless Helpful Tidbit 11:** China's National Sword policy, implemented in 2018, banned the import of 24 types of solid waste, forcing many countries to improve their recycling infrastructure.

**Useless Helpful Tidbit 12:** In 2019, the world generated about 53.6 million metric tons of e-waste, but only 17.4% was recycled properly.

**Useless Helpful Tidbit 13:** The United Nations estimates that global electronic waste could increase by 38% between 2020 and 2030, emphasizing the need for better recycling systems.

**Useless Helpful Tidbit 14:** In 2018, the recycling rate for glass in the European Union was 76%, one of the highest rates for any material.

**Useless Helpful Tidbit 15:** The implementation of recycling programs in South Korea has led to a recycling rate of 59% for municipal waste, significantly reducing landfill use.

**Useless Helpful Tidbit 16:** Italy's municipal waste recycling rate is 51.3%, driven by solid regional policies and public awareness campaigns.

**Useless Helpful Tidbit 17:** To transition to a circular economy, the UK aims to recycle 65% of its municipal waste by 2035.

**Useless Helpful Tidbit 18:** Norway's efficient bottle deposit system has led to a recycling rate of over 97% for plastic bottles, setting a global standard.

**Useless Helpful Tidbit 19:** The National Waste Policy Action Plan aims to achieve an 80% average recovery rate from all waste streams in Australia by 2030.

**Useless Helpful Tidbit 20:** The World Bank estimates that by improving waste management practices, countries could reduce global emissions by up to 20% by 2050.

## Great Big Grab Bag of Fun Factoids

**Fun Factoid 1:** Recycling just one aluminum can saves enough energy to power a television for three hours.

**Fun Factoid 2:** The global recycling industry is valued at over $500 billion, reflecting its significant economic impact.

**Fun Factoid 3:** In 2020, the EU recycled nearly 70% of its packaging waste, making it one of the most prosperous regions for recycling efforts.

**Fun Factoid 4:** The United Nations launched the Clean Seas campaign in 2017, aiming to significantly reduce marine plastic pollution through improved recycling and waste management.

**Fun Factoid 5:** The energy saved from recycling glass bottles in the United States in one year is enough to power a city the size of Dallas for almost a year.

# Chapter 6: The Reality of Collected Recyclables

Recycling is more than just tossing items into the bin—it involves a complex journey from collection to processing. Despite our best efforts, not all items in recycling bins are successfully recycled. Understanding what happens to these materials can help us improve our recycling practices and reduce waste.

**What Happens to Items in the Recycling Bin**

Once recyclables are collected, they are transported to material recovery facilities (MRFs), where they are sorted, cleaned, and processed. Items are separated by type—paper, plastic, metal, and glass—using a combination of manual labor and automated machinery. Contaminated items, such as food-soiled paper or non-recyclable plastics, can spoil entire batches, reducing the overall efficiency of recycling programs.

**The Journey of Recyclables from Collection to Processing**

At MRFs, recyclables undergo several stages of sorting. First, materials are loaded onto conveyor belts where large items like cardboard are removed. Magnets extract metals, air classifiers separate lightweight plastics, and optical scanners identify and sort different types of plastics. The sorted materials are then baled and sold to manufacturers who use them to produce new products. However, the journey doesn't always end here—some contaminated materials might be diverted to landfills.

**The Percentage of Collected Items That Are Successfully Recycled**

The success rate of recycling varies widely depending on the material and region. For instance, aluminum and steel have high recycling rates of around 70-90% due to their value and ease of processing. In contrast, plastic recycling rates are significantly lower, with only about 8-9% of all plastic waste recycled globally. Contamination and the lack of market demand for certain materials contribute to these low rates.

## Grab Bag of Useless Helpful Tidbits on the Fate of Recyclables

1. **Aluminum Advantage**: Aluminum cans are one of the most recyclable items, with nearly 75% of all aluminum ever produced still in use today.
2. **Glass Cycle**: Glass can be recycled indefinitely without losing quality, yet only about 33% of glass containers are recycled in the U.S.
3. **Plastic Predicament**: Only about 9% of all plastic ever produced has been recycled, mainly due to the complexity and cost of processing.
4. **Paper Trail**: Paper recycling is highly efficient, with about 66% of paper products being recycled, though this varies by region.
5. **E-Waste Challenge**: Electronic waste is a growing concern, with only 20% of global e-waste being formally recycled.
6. **Contamination Crisis**: Approximately 25% of items in recycling bins are contaminated to the point of being non-recyclable.

7. **China's Policy Impact**: In 2018, China's National Sword policy banned the import of most plastics and other materials, disrupting global recycling systems.

8. **Composting Confusion**: Items like pizza boxes are often recyclable only if they are free of food residue and grease.

9. **Wishcycling Woes**: Tossing non-recyclable items in the bin with the hope they will be recycled often leads to more contamination.

10. **Ocean Plastics**: It is estimated that 8 million tons of plastic enter the oceans annually, highlighting the need for better recycling practices.

11. **Textile Trouble**: Textile recycling is complicated, with only about 15% of discarded clothing recycled.

12. **Metal Magic**: Steel is the most recycled material in the world, with over 80% being recycled annually.

13. **Municipal Myths**: Many municipalities struggle with the cost of recycling programs, often relying on taxpayer subsidies.

14. **Upcycling Innovations**: Creative upcycling projects transform waste materials into new, often artistic, products.

15. **Lifecycle Loopholes**: Some items, like black plastic, are not detected by recycling sorting systems and often end up in landfills.

16. **Recycling Symbols**: A recycling symbol on packaging doesn't always mean the item is recyclable.

17. **Bottle Bills**: States with bottle deposit laws see higher recycling rates for beverage containers.

18. **Recycled Roads**: Some recycled plastics are used in

road construction, offering sustainable use for otherwise hard-to-recycle materials.

19. **Circular Economy**: The concept of a circular economy aims to design out waste and keep materials in use as long as possible.

20. **Global Disparities**: Recycling rates vary significantly worldwide, with some countries achieving over 90% recycling rates while others lag far behind.


## Great Big Grab Bag of Fun Factoids

1. **Surprising Success**: Sweden recycles nearly 99% of its household waste, with only 1% ending up in landfills.

2. **Landfill Laws**: In Switzerland, it's illegal to dispose of recyclable materials in regular trash, contributing to its high recycling rates.

3. **Recycling Revenue**: The recycling industry generates over $100 billion annually in the United States alone.

4. **Plastic Paradox**: If current trends continue, the ocean's plastic amount is expected to outweigh all the fish by 2050.

5. **Biodegradable Misconceptions**: Many items labeled as biodegradable require specific conditions to decompose, often not met in standard landfills.

# Chapter 7: Recycling Misconceptions

**Items Commonly Thought to be Recyclable but Aren't**

While recycling seems straightforward, many items that appear to be recyclable are not accepted in curbside bins. For instance, greasy pizza boxes, plastic bags, and certain types of glass like mirrors and Pyrex are often mistakenly tossed in with recyclables, causing contamination and processing issues.

**The Confusion Surrounding Recycling Symbols and Labels**

Recycling symbols and labels can be misleading. The presence of the recycling symbol doesn't always mean an item is recyclable. Numbers inside the symbol indicate the type of plastic but don't guarantee that local facilities can process it. Compostable and biodegradable labels add to the confusion, as these materials require specific conditions to break down and are unsuitable for standard recycling bins.

**Examples of Recycling Fails and Misconceptions**

Recycling programs frequently suffer from well-intentioned but misguided efforts known as "wish cycling," which involves placing non-recyclable items in the recycling bin hoping to be recycled. Examples include plastic straws, Styrofoam, and certain electronics. These items can contaminate loads, leading to more waste sent to landfills.

**Grab Bag of Useless Helpful Tidbits**

1. **Plastic Bags**: Most curbside programs don't accept

plastic bags, which can jam sorting machinery.

2. **Greasy Pizza Boxes**: Food residue makes greasy pizza boxes non-recyclable; only clean parts can be recycled.

3. **Shredded Paper**: Although paper is recyclable, shredded paper often isn't due to the small size of the pieces.

4. **Bottle Caps**: Small items like bottle caps are usually not recyclable unless attached to the bottle.

5. **Ceramics and Pyrex**: These items aren't recyclable because they have different melting points than standard glass.

6. **Coffee Cups**: Disposable coffee cups are often lined with plastic, making them difficult to recycle.

7. **Receipts**: Thermal paper receipts contain chemicals that make them unsuitable for recycling.

8. **Styrofoam**: While technically recyclable, Styrofoam is not accepted by most curbside programs due to its low density and high contamination risk.

9. **Plastic Utensils**: Many recycling facilities don't accept plastic utensils because they are too small and often made from low-grade plastic.

10. **Hoses and Wires**: Items like garden hoses and electrical wires can tangle in sorting machinery and are not recyclable.

11. **Biodegradable Plastics**: These require industrial composting facilities and can't be processed with regular recyclables.

12. **Clothing and Textiles**: Most curbside programs don't accept textiles requiring specialized recycling methods.

13. **Mirror Glass**: Mirrors contain coatings that make

them non-recyclable with regular glass.

14. **Aerosol Cans**: Unless empty, aerosol cans are dangerous and are typically not accepted in curbside recycling.

15. **Paper Towels and Tissues**: These items are often contaminated with food or bodily fluids and are not recyclable.

16. **Black Plastic**: Many sorting systems can't detect black plastic, so it's often not recycled.

17. **Plastic Toys**: Toys are made from mixed plastics and other materials, complicating recycling.

18. **Foil Packaging**: Items like chip bags are often made from mixed materials, making them non-recyclable.

19. **CDs and DVDs**: These are not accepted in curbside recycling and require special handling.

20. **Disposable Diapers**: These are not recyclable due to their complex material composition and contamination.

## Great Big Grab Bag of Fun Factoids

1. **"Wishcycling" Phenomenon**: About 25% of all items placed in recycling bins in the U.S. are contaminated by non-recyclable materials due to "wishcycling."

2. **Recycling Symbol Confusion**: Over 50% of people mistakenly believe a recycling symbol means an item is recyclable in their local program.

3. **Plastic Recycling Codes**: There are seven different plastic recycling codes, but not all are accepted in all

programs, leading to significant confusion.

4. **Biodegradable Plastics Issue**: Biodegradable plastics can contaminate recycling streams and require different processing conditions than traditional plastics.

5. **E-Waste Misconception**: Many people are unaware that electronic waste requires special recycling procedures, leading to improper disposal in curbside bins.

# Chapter 8: Innovative Recycling Technologies

**New Technologies and Methods in Recycling**

The recycling industry constantly evolves, with new technologies and methods being developed to improve efficiency and effectiveness. Innovations such as advanced sorting systems, chemical recycling, and biodegradable materials are transforming the landscape. These technologies aim to address the limitations of traditional recycling processes and handle a wider variety of materials more efficiently.

**The Future of Recycling and Sustainable Waste Management**

As we move towards a more sustainable future, the recycling industry is expected to play a crucial role in waste management. The future of recycling includes a greater emphasis on circular economy principles, where materials are kept in use for as long as possible. Advances in technology will make it easier to recycle complex materials and reduce the environmental impact of waste.

**Case Studies of Cutting-Edge Recycling Innovations**

Numerous projects and initiatives worldwide are showcasing the potential of innovative recycling technologies. From robotic sorting systems in Norway to chemical recycling plants in Japan, these case studies highlight the diverse approaches to tackling recycling challenges. These projects demonstrate the technical feasibility of new methods and their economic and environmental benefits.

## Grab Bag of Useless Helpful Tidbits

1. **Robotic Sorting Systems**: Advanced robots equipped with AI and machine learning are revolutionizing sorting facilities by identifying and separating materials more accurately than humans.
2. **Chemical Recycling**: This process breaks down plastics into their chemical components, allowing the recycling of mixed and contaminated plastics that are otherwise unrecyclable.
3. **Pyrolysis**: A thermal decomposition process that converts plastic waste into synthetic oil, which can be used as a fuel or further processed into new plastics.
4. **Biodegradable Plastics**: New biodegradable plastics are being developed to break down in natural environments without leaving harmful residues.
5. **Closed-Loop Recycling**: Systems where waste materials are collected, processed, and reused to create the same product, such as aluminum cans.
6. **Smart Bins**: Equipped with sensors and IoT technology, Smart bins can sort recyclables automatically and provide data on recycling habits.
7. **Graphene from Waste**: Researchers have developed methods to convert plastic waste into graphene, a valuable material in various high-tech applications.
8. **Microbial Recycling**: Utilizing bacteria and fungi to break down complex plastics into simpler compounds that can be reused.
9. **Ocean Plastic Cleanup**: Innovations like The Ocean Cleanup project aim to remove plastic waste from

oceans and recycle it into new products.

10. **Upcycling Innovations**: Turning waste materials into higher-value products, such as fashion items made from recycled textiles.

11. **Waste-to-Energy Plants**: Facilities that convert non-recyclable waste into energy through incineration and gasification.

12. **Advanced Composite Recycling**: Technologies that separate and recycle composite materials like carbon fiber and fiberglass.

13. **Recycling of Rare Earth Metals**: New methods to extract and recycle rare earth elements from electronic waste.

14. **3D Printing with Recycled Materials**: Using recycled plastics and other materials as feedstock for 3D printing.

15. **Plastic-to-Fuel Conversion**: Processes that convert plastic waste into diesel and other fuels.

16. **Hydrothermal Liquefaction**: A process that converts organic waste, including plastics, into crude oil using high temperatures and pressure.

17. **Artificial Intelligence in Recycling**: AI algorithms that optimize sorting and processing operations to increase recycling rates.

18. **Nano-Enhanced Materials**: Using nanotechnology to create more recyclable and sustainable materials.

19. **Circular Fashion**: Clothing lines are designed to be fully recyclable or compostable at the end of their life cycle.

20. **Blockchain for Recycling**: Implementing blockchain

technology to track and verify the recycling process, ensuring transparency and efficiency.

## Great Big Grab Bag of Fun Factoids

1.  **Robotic Efficiency**: Robotic sorting systems can process recyclables at 80 items per minute, significantly higher than human workers' 40 items per minute.
2.  **Chemical Recycling Potential**: Chemical recycling could recycle up to 90% of all plastic waste, compared to the current mechanical recycling rate of about 9%.
3.  **Smart Bins Impact**: Smart bins equipped with AI and IoT technology can increase recycling rates by up to 30% by reducing contamination and improving sorting accuracy.
4.  **Ocean Cleanup Success**: The Ocean Cleanup project has removed over 1,000 tons of plastic from the Great Pacific Garbage Patch, highlighting the potential for large-scale ocean plastic recovery.
5.  **3D Printing Revolution**: Using recycled materials, 3D printing could reduce plastic waste by up to 80%, offering a sustainable alternative for manufacturing.

# Chapter 9: The Global Waste Crisis

**The Scale and Impact of the Global Waste Problem**

The global waste crisis is a pressing environmental issue, with the world generating over 2 billion tons of municipal solid waste annually. This staggering garbage has significant ecological, social, and economic impacts, including pollution, greenhouse gas emissions, and health hazards. Landfill overflow and improper waste disposal contaminate soil and water, affecting ecosystems and human health.

**Recycling as a Solution to the Waste Crisis**

Recycling is critical in mitigating the global waste crisis by diverting waste from landfills and reducing the need for virgin materials. Effective recycling programs can significantly lower greenhouse gas emissions, conserve natural resources, and reduce energy consumption. However, recycling alone cannot solve the entire problem and must be part of a broader waste management strategy that includes reduction, reuse, and responsible consumption.

**Comparative Analysis of Recycling and Other Waste Management Strategies**

To address the waste crisis, various waste management strategies are employed worldwide, including landfilling, incineration, composting, and recycling. Each method has its pros and cons. For example, while landfilling is common, it often leads to long-term environmental issues. Incineration reduces waste volume but can produce harmful emissions. Composting is effective for organic waste but not for other materials. Recycling, though beneficial, requires proper infrastructure and public participation to be effective. A comprehensive approach combining these strategies is essential for sustainable waste management.


## Grab Bag of Useless Helpful Tidbits

1. **Global Waste Generation**: The world generates over 2 billion tons of municipal solid waste yearly, with high-income countries contributing about 34%.
2. **Plastic Waste**: Approximately 300 million tons of plastic waste are produced annually, with only 9% recycled.
3. **Landfill Impact**: Landfills are the third-largest source of human-related methane emissions, a potent greenhouse gas.
4. **Ocean Pollution**: Over 8 million tons of plastic enter the oceans annually, contributing to massive "garbage patches" in ocean gyres.
5. **E-Waste Growth**: E-waste is the fastest-growing waste stream, with over 50 million tons generated annually and only 20% formally recycled.
6. **Textile Waste**: The fashion industry generates about 92 million tons of textile waste each year, of which less than 1% is recycled into new garments.
7. **Food Waste**: Nearly one-third of all food produced globally is wasted, amounting to 1.3 billion tons annually.
8. **Recycling Rates**: Europe leads in recycling rates, with countries like Germany recycling over 65% of their

waste.

9. **Incineration**: Some countries, such as Japan and Sweden, extensively use waste-to-energy incineration, converting waste into electricity and heat.

10. **Composting Success**: San Francisco diverts about 80% of its waste from landfills through extensive composting and recycling programs.

11. **Packaging Waste**: Packaging accounts for about 40% of global plastic production and a significant portion of waste.

12. **Landfill Lifespan**: Many landfills are reaching capacity, leading to the search for new sites or alternative waste management solutions.

13. **Global Recycling Market**: The global recycling market is valued at over $200 billion, driven by increasing waste generation and environmental concerns.

14. **Circular Economy**: The circular economy concept aims to minimize waste by keeping products and materials in use for as long as possible.

15. **Biodegradable Confusion**: Many items labeled as biodegradable require specific conditions to break down and do not decompose quickly in landfills.

16. **Extended Producer Responsibility (EPR)**: EPR policies hold manufacturers accountable for the entire lifecycle of their products, including disposal and recycling.

17. **Single-Use Plastics Ban**: Several countries have implemented bans on single-use plastics to reduce waste and pollution.

18. **Waste Export**: Some countries export their waste to developing nations, raising ethical and environmental concerns.
19. **Recycling Jobs**: The recycling industry supports millions of jobs worldwide, contributing to economic growth.
20. **Zero Waste Movement**: The Zero Waste movement advocates for reducing waste generation to near zero through sustainable practices.

**Great Big Grab Bag of Fun Factoids**

1. **Landfill Proliferation**: If current trends continue, the world could face a landfill space crisis by 2050, with no more room to dispose of waste.
2. **Plastic in the Ocean**: If no significant changes are made, by 2050, there could be more plastic in the oceans by weight than fish.
3. **E-Waste Gold**: It is estimated that the e-waste discarded each year contains precious metals worth over $60 billion.
4. **Food Waste Emissions**: If food waste were a country, it would be the third-largest emitter of greenhouse gases after the U.S. and China.
5. **Recycling Potential**: Recycling the world's recyclable waste could save enough energy to power 1 billion homes annually.

# Chapter 10: The Dark Side of Recycling

While recycling is often hailed as an environmental savior, it also has a darker side that deserves attention. One major issue arose in 2018 when China, previously the world's largest importer of recyclable waste, implemented a ban on importing most plastics and other materials. This policy shift forced Western countries to find new recyclable destinations, leading to a surge of exports to Southeast Asian nations such as Malaysia, Indonesia, and Vietnam. Unfortunately, these countries often lack the infrastructure to manage the influx, resulting in significant environmental damage, including illegal dumping and ocean pollution.

The environmental costs of recycling are not limited to improper waste management. The process itself can have a substantial carbon footprint. Collecting, transporting, and processing recyclables consume energy and resources, sometimes offsetting the environmental benefits. Additionally, contamination in recycling streams can render large batches of materials non-recyclable, ultimately diverting them to landfills and diminishing the efficiency of recycling programs.

E-waste, or electronic waste, presents another dark aspect of recycling. If not correctly handled, E-waste contains hazardous materials such as lead, mercury, and cadmium, posing severe environmental and health risks. Much of the world's e-waste is shipped to countries with less stringent environmental regulations, where informal recycling sectors dismantle and process it in unsafe conditions. This not only endangers workers but also leads to the release of toxic substances into the environment.

Economic disparities further complicate the global recycling landscape. Market instabilities and fluctuating prices for recycled materials can make recycling programs financially unsustainable. Developing countries, which often become the dumping grounds for the world's recyclables, suffer from environmental degradation and health issues due to insufficient waste management infrastructure. These nations bear the brunt of the environmental and social costs associated with the global recycling trade, highlighting the need for more equitable and sustainable practices.

In summary, while recycling has its benefits, these darker aspects reveal a complex and often troubling reality. Addressing these issues requires comprehensive solutions encompassing policy changes, improved infrastructure, and global cooperation to ensure that recycling benefits the environment and society.

**Grab Bag of Useless Helpful Tidbits**

- **Useless Helpful Tidbit 1:** After China banned plastic waste imports, the U.S. and Europe shifted their exports to Southeast Asia, causing environmental crises in countries like Malaysia and Indonesia.
- **Useless Helpful Tidbit 2:** Recycling's carbon footprint can sometimes outweigh its benefits, especially when recyclables are transported long distances.
- **Useless Helpful Tidbit 3:** Contaminated recyclables can cause entire batches to be landfilled, with contamination rates as high as 25% in some programs.

- **Useless Helpful Tidbit 4:** Informal e-waste recycling in Ghana and India exposes workers to dangerous chemicals, impacting their health and the local environment.
- **Useless Helpful Tidbit 5:** The price of recycled materials can fluctuate wildly, making it difficult for recycling programs to remain economically viable.
- **Useless Helpful Tidbit 6:** In 2019, a shipment of 1,500 tons of waste from Australia was found improperly labeled as recyclable and returned by Indonesia.
- **Useless Helpful Tidbit 7:** Only about 20% of global e-waste is formally recycled, with the rest often ending up in landfills or informal recycling operations.
- **Useless Helpful Tidbit 8:** The energy required to collect, transport, and process recyclables can be substantial, sometimes rivaling the energy savings from recycling.
- **Useless Helpful Tidbit 9:** Illegal dumping of recyclables has been reported off the coasts of developing countries, where enforcement of environmental laws is weak.
- **Useless Helpful Tidbit 10:** Recycling programs in some cities face budget cuts due to economic downturns, leading to reduced effectiveness and increased waste.
- **Useless Helpful Tidbit 11:** Improperly managed waste imports can lead to severe pollution problems, as seen in countries like Malaysia after China's import

ban.

- **Useless Helpful Tidbit 12:** E-waste contains precious metals like gold and silver, making it a lucrative but hazardous sector for informal recyclers.
- **Useless Helpful Tidbit 13:** The Basel Convention aims to control hazardous waste movements, but enforcement remains challenging, especially for e-waste.
- **Useless Helpful Tidbit 14:** In 2018, Malaysia sent back 150 containers of illegal plastic waste to their countries of origin, highlighting the global issue of waste dumping.
- **Useless Helpful Tidbit 15:** Informal recycling sectors often lack proper safety equipment, leading to significant health risks for workers handling hazardous materials.
- **Useless Helpful Tidbit 16:** Recycling market instabilities can lead to material stockpiling, which can cause storage and environmental problems.
- **Useless Helpful Tidbit 17:** Developing countries often lack the infrastructure to manage the large volumes of imported waste, leading to widespread environmental degradation.
- **Useless Helpful Tidbit 18:** Some developed countries have invested in domestic recycling infrastructure to reduce reliance on exporting waste.
- **Useless Helpful Tidbit 19:** The informal recycling sector employs over 15 million people worldwide, often in hazardous and unregulated conditions.

- **Useless Helpful Tidbit 20:** The actual environmental cost of recycling must consider both the benefits and the negative impacts of improper waste management practices.

## Great Big Grab Bag of Fun Factoids

- **Fun Factoid 1:** Only 9% of all plastic ever produced has been recycled, with the rest ending up in landfills or the natural environment.
- **Fun Factoid 2:** The informal recycling sector employs over 15 million people worldwide, often in hazardous and unregulated conditions.
- **Fun Factoid 3:** The Basel Convention aims to control the transboundary movements of hazardous wastes, including e-waste, but enforcement remains challenging.
- **Fun Factoid 4:** In 2018, Malaysia sent back 150 containers of illegal plastic waste to their countries of origin, highlighting the global issue of waste dumping.
- **Fun Factoid 5:** The World Bank estimates that global waste could increase by 70% by 2050 without significant changes, exacerbating existing recycling challenges.

# Your Great Big Grab Bag of Useless Trivia

Welcome to the weird and wonderful world of recycling trivia! Prepare yourself for a whirlwind tour of bizarre facts, strange practices, and unusual products that have emerged from the recycling revolution. From the quirky to the downright mind-boggling, this chapter will surely entertain and inform with its collection of 50 unique tidbits; each expanded into a humorous narrative.

### 1. The Great Garment Gobbler

Did you know that your old jeans might end up insulating someone's home? Denim is increasingly being recycled into eco-friendly insulation material. It's cozy and effective, and it makes you wonder how many pairs of jeans it takes to keep a house warm. Imagine the insulation shouting, "We're here to protect your home, one Levi's at a time!"

### 2. Bottle Cap Bonanza

Have you ever tried making an art piece out of bottle caps? In Kenya, artists are turning discarded bottle caps into vibrant, colorful mosaics. These stunning creations not only beautify public spaces but also highlight the creative potential of what we often consider trash. Picasso might just roll over in his grave—in jealousy.

### 3. The Cardboard Cathedral

Christchurch, New Zealand, built an entire cathedral out of cardboard. After an earthquake destroyed the original, they constructed a temporary church from 98 cardboard tubes. It's a testament to the strength and versatility of cardboard – and to the faith that recycling can hold up the heavens (or at least a roof).

### 4. Rubber Road Warriors

Have you ever wondered where old tires go to die? Many end up reincarnated as road surfaces. Some highways are paved with rubberized asphalt made from recycled tires. It's a smooth ride and helps reduce road noise, giving your car's suspension a break and your ears some peace.

### 5. Pencil with a Twist

What happens to those tiny pencil stubs that are too short to use? One innovative company recycles them into new pencils. But here's the twist – these pencils have a seed capsule at the end. Once you're done writing your magnum opus, you can plant the pencil and grow a tree. The circle of life continues, pencil-style.

### 6. Glass Gravel

In a clever twist, crushed glass is used as gravel in construction projects. It's a practical building material and a great way to repurpose the mountains of glass bottles we discard. Walk on glass? It's more like driving on glass, without a worry in the world.

### 7. Fleece from the Sea

Believe it or not, those cozy fleece jackets can be made from recycled plastic bottles. Brands like Patagonia have been turning old plastic into new clothing for years. So next time you're bundled up against the cold, remember: you're wearing yesterday's soda bottles. Cheers to that!

### 8. Coffee to Compost

Used coffee grounds are being collected and converted into biofuel and compost in some cities. Not only does this reduce waste, but it also creates a renewable energy source. The next time you sip your latte, take a moment to appreciate how your morning joe could eventually help power a city bus.

### 9. Grease to Diesel

Old cooking oil is being transformed into biodiesel, a cleaner alternative to fossil fuels. Your favorite French fries might have been cooked in oil fueling a truck. It's the ultimate greasy hand-me-down, where yesterday's meal helps transport today's goods.

### 10. E-Waste Jewelry

Discarded electronics are a goldmine – literally. Precious metals like gold, silver, and platinum are extracted from e-waste and used to make jewelry. The next time you admire a shiny necklace, it might be made from an old phone. Talk about tech bling!

### 11. Recycled Runners

Nike's "Grind" program turns old athletic shoes into materials for new sports surfaces and playgrounds. So, if your worn-out sneakers had dreams of making it to the big leagues, they just might – under the feet of future Olympians.

### 12. Ship Shape

Old ships don't just sail off into the sunset. They're often dismantled and their materials recycled. Steel from decommissioned ships can be reused in construction, giving these maritime giants a second life as skyscrapers or bridges.

### 13. Trashy Tunes

Musicians in Paraguay's Cateura landfill have created an entire orchestra using instruments made from recycled materials. Violins from oil cans, flutes from water pipes – it's a testament to the beauty that can be found in trash. Mozart would be proud.

### 14. Paper with a Past

Some companies are producing paper products from recycled paper so efficiently that the result is almost indistinguishable from new paper. Your following office memo might be made from a previous bestseller. Hopefully, it's as enjoyable as the original.

### 15. The Rise of Recycled Roads

Plastic waste is transformed into road-building materials in India and the Netherlands. These plastic roads are more durable and less prone to potholes. It's a smooth, sustainable solution – turning our throwaway culture into thoroughfares.

### 16. Green Games

The Tokyo 2020 Olympic medals were made from recycled electronics. The gold, silver, and bronze were sourced from old phones, laptops, and other gadgets. Athletes weren't just competing for glory – they were winning a piece of recycled history.

### 17. Fishing Net Footwear

Adidas has partnered with Parley for the Oceans to create shoes made from recycled ocean plastics, including discarded fishing nets. So, next time you lace up your sneakers, you might be giving marine life a breather. Fishy fashion has never been more relaxed.

### 18. From Trash to Toilets

In some developing countries, waste plastic is converted into affordable, durable toilet structures. These eco-friendly facilities improve sanitation and reduce plastic pollution. It's a throne fit for sustainability royalty.

### 19. Brick by Recycled Brick

Plastic waste is being turned into bricks for construction in innovative projects worldwide. These plastic bricks are lightweight, durable, and cheap to produce. They might pave the way to a more sustainable building industry.

### 20. Eco-Brick Benches

In South Africa, eco-bricks – plastic bottles stuffed with non-recyclable waste – are used to create park benches. These sturdy seats offer a place to rest and a reminder of the creative potential in every piece of trash.

### 21. Solar-Powered Trash Compactors

Some cities have installed solar-powered trash compactors that can hold up to five times more waste than regular bins. They even notify waste management when they're full. It's trash-talking with a tech twist.

### 22. Fashion Forward

H&M's Conscious Collection features clothing made from recycled fabrics and materials. Fast fashion meets sustainable chic, proving that looking good and doing good can go hand in hand.

### 23. Waste-Powered WiFi

Public WiFi hotspots are powered by waste-to-energy technology in parts of New York City. The trash you throw away might help you browse the internet. Talk about staying connected!

### 24. Recycled Skyscrapers

The Shanghai Tower, one of the tallest buildings in the world, used over 20% recycled materials in its construction. It's a towering testament to the potential of sustainable architecture.

### 25. Printer Cartridges to Paving

Some companies are recycling used printer cartridges into materials for road construction. So, the next time you replace your ink, you might be helping pave the way for a new highway.

### 26. Musical Marine Debris

Artists are creating musical instruments from marine debris collected from the ocean. These unique instruments raise awareness about ocean pollution while producing beautiful music. It's recycling that hits all the right notes.

### 27. Recycled Art Installations

Art installations worldwide are made from recycled materials, turning trash into treasure. These works of art challenge perceptions and inspire conversations about sustainability.

### 28. Second-Life Satellites

Old satellites are being repurposed into new space technology. This approach reduces space junk and gives these old satellites a new lease on life. Space recycling – it's out of this world!

### 29. Green Gadgets

Companies like Apple create devices from recycled materials, including aluminum and rare earth elements. Your next iPhone might have a past life as another iPhone. It's a high-tech reincarnation.

### 30. Tire Playgrounds

Old tires are being transformed into playground surfaces and structures, providing a safe and fun environment for kids while keeping tires out of landfills. Bounce back with some tire-inspired fun!

### 31. Floating Gardens

In Bangladesh, floating gardens made from water hyacinth and other plant materials are used to cultivate crops. These sustainable gardens provide food security and utilize waste materials effectively.

### 32. Cardboard Coffins

Eco-friendly cardboard coffins are becoming a popular choice for green funerals. They're biodegradable, customizable, and significantly less costly than traditional caskets. Recycling takes on an eternal perspective.

### 33. Recycled Road Signs

In the UK, old road signs are being recycled into new ones. It's a circular journey for these directional aids, guiding us towards a more sustainable future.

### 34. Plastic-Eating Fungi

Researchers have discovered fungi that can break down plastic, offering a potential natural solution to plastic pollution. These tiny decomposers are nature's unsung heroes, munching their way through our waste.

### 35. Repurposed Pillows

Companies are making pillows and bedding from recycled materials, including plastic bottles. Sleep tight, knowing you're resting your head on yesterday's recycling.

### 36. Library of Things

Some communities have established "Libraries of Things," where people can borrow items like tools, kitchen appliances, and sports equipment. This reduces waste and promotes sharing, turning community spirit into a tangible resource.

### 37. Biodegradable Bubble Wrap

Eco-friendly bubble wrap made from biodegradable materials cushion packages with care for the environment. Next time you pop bubble wrap, you're making a sustainable impact – one satisfying pop at a time.

### 38. Compostable Cutlery

Cutlery made from cornstarch and other plant-based materials is compostable and offers an eco-friendly alternative to plastic. Dinner parties just got a green upgrade, one fork at a time.

### 39. Streetwear from Street Trash

Streetwear brands are using recycled materials to create fashion statements. From discarded street signs to old billboards, urban waste is transformed into high-fashion pieces.

### 40. Plastic-Free Packaging

Innovative companies are developing packaging from materials like mushroom mycelium and seaweed. These alternatives are biodegradable and reduce our reliance on plastic.

### 41. Reclaimed Wood Wonders

Old barns and buildings are dismantled, and the wood is repurposed for new construction projects. This reclaimed wood brings history and character to modern spaces.

### 42. Waste to Wealth

In some developing countries, waste pickers are crucial to recycling efforts. They collect, sort, and sell recyclables, making trash a livelihood and contributing to the economy.

### 43. Solar Panel Recycling

With the rise of solar energy, there's also a growing need to recycle solar panels. New technologies are emerging to recover valuable materials from old panels, ensuring a sustainable energy cycle.

### 44. Trashy Trophies

Recycling competitions and events often award trophies made from recycled materials. Winning an accolade that symbolizes sustainability is a prize worth cherishing.

### 45. The Eco-Friendly Toothbrush

Biodegradable toothbrushes made from bamboo and recycled plastics are gaining popularity. They keep your teeth clean and your conscience clear.

## 46. Upcycled Upholstery

Furniture manufacturers use recycled materials for upholstery, creating stylish and sustainable home decor. Sitting pretty has never been so environmentally friendly.

## 47. Green Graffiti

Artists are using moss and other natural materials to create eco-friendly graffiti. These living artworks promote sustainability while adding a green touch to urban landscapes.

## 48. Beer Bottle Bricks

Some innovative construction projects are using recycled beer bottles as building materials. These "bottle bricks" add a unique aesthetic and reduce waste.

## 49. Waste-Based Biofuel

Researchers are converting organic waste into biofuel, offering a renewable energy source that helps manage waste. It's a win-win for energy and the environment.

## 50. Paper Pencils

Some companies are making pencils from recycled paper, reducing the need for wood. These paper pencils write just as well, giving a new purpose to old newspapers and magazines.

# Highlights and Key Takeaways

We've journeyed through the complex and fascinating world of recycling, exploring everything from the basics of what happens to your recyclables to the latest innovations transforming waste management. Here are some key highlights and takeaways:

- **Understanding Recycling Processes**: We've demystified what happens to items in your recycling bin and their complex journey from collection to processing.
- **Recycling Misconceptions**: We debunked common myths and clarified what can and cannot be recycled, helping you become a more informed recycler.
- **Innovative Technologies**: We explored cutting-edge recycling technologies, from robotic sorting systems to chemical recycling, that are paving the way for a more sustainable future.
- **Global Waste Crisis**: We examined the scale of the global waste problem and how recycling can play a vital role in mitigating its impact.
- **Fun and Quirky Trivia**: We indulged in a delightful array of recycling trivia, discovering the weird and beautiful ways waste is repurposed worldwide.

# Learn More

Recycling constantly evolves, and there is always more to learn and explore. By staying informed and proactive, you can make a significant impact on reducing waste and promoting sustainability in your community. We encourage you to dive deeper into the topics we've covered and continue your journey towards becoming an eco-warrior.

**Additional Resources**

For those eager to expand their knowledge and stay updated on the latest developments in recycling and waste management, here are some valuable resources:

**Books**

1. **"Plastic Free: How I Kicked the Plastic Habit and How You Can Too" by Beth Terry**: A practical guide to reducing plastic use daily.
2. **"Garbology: Our Dirty Love Affair with Trash" by Edward Humes**: An eye-opening exploration of America's waste problem and innovative solutions.
3. **"Cradle to Cradle: Remaking the Way We Make Things" by William McDonough and Michael Braungart**: A seminal work on sustainable design and the circular economy.

**Websites**

1. **Earth911 (www.earth911.com[1])**: A comprehensive resource for recycling information, including a search

---

1. http://www.earth911.com

tool for local recycling options.

2. **Recycle Now (www.recyclenow.com[2]):** The UK's national recycling campaign with tips and information on recycling effectively.
3. **The Ellen MacArthur Foundation (www.ellenmacarthurfoundation.org[3]):** An organization dedicated to promoting the circular economy through innovation and education.

## Organizations and Initiatives

1. **The Ocean Cleanup (www.theoceancleanup.com[4]):** An initiative focused on removing plastic from the oceans and rivers.
2. **Greenpeace (www.greenpeace.org[5]):** An environmental organization that campaigns for sustainable waste management and reducing plastic pollution.
3. **Zero Waste International Alliance (www.zwia.org[6]):** A global network advocating for zero waste and sustainable resource management principles.

## Documentaries

1. **"A Plastic Ocean"** is a documentary exploring the

---

2. http://www.recyclenow.com

3. http://www.ellenmacarthurfoundation.org

4. http://www.theoceancleanup.com

5. http://www.greenpeace.org

6. http://www.zwia.org

devastating impact of plastic pollution on marine life and ecosystems.

2. **"The Story of Stuff"**: A short film and ongoing project that examines the lifecycle of goods and promotes sustainable consumption.

3. **"Wasted! The Story of Food Waste"**: A documentary that looks at the environmental impact of food waste and innovative solutions to reduce it.

By exploring these resources, you can stay informed about the latest trends, technologies, and recycling and waste management strategies. Every small step counts and your efforts to recycle more effectively and reduce waste can contribute to a healthier, more sustainable planet. Happy recycling!

# Don't miss out!

Visit the website below and you can sign up to receive emails whenever Michael Clutton publishes a new book. There's no charge and no obligation.

https://books2read.com/r/B-A-IAFJB-VSMPD

**BOOKS 2 READ**

Connecting independent readers to independent writers.

Did you love *300 Trashy Truths You Didn't Need to Know*? Then you should read *Religions of the World*[7] by Michael P. Clutton!

**Discover the Sacred, the Strange, and Everything in Between A Journey Through Humanity's Spiritual Spectrum**Explore the multifaceted world of spiritual beliefs in our Grab Bag of Information about the Religions of the World. More than just a stats book, or a trivia book. This one has all that and more! Your Great Big Grab Bag is your great big passport to a vivid exploration of the world's religious tapestry—from mainstream faiths to the more obscure pseudo-religions. Engage with tales of oddities, contradictions, and the unifying threads that

7. https://books2read.com/u/mB1L0N

8. https://books2read.com/u/mB1L0N

intertwine through practices both ancient and modern. Whether it's the comic mix-up of holy texts leading to accidental pastry worship or the serene yet complex rituals of the Eastern philosophies, this book offers a kaleidoscope of vignettes and factoids that entertain as much as they enlighten. Navigate through practices that mold societies, inspire billions, and even spark controversies. With each chapter, gain insights into how these diverse belief systems shape the human experience, echoing the common quest for deeper meaning. Perfect for the curious mind, this guide ensures every reader will come away with a broader, and perhaps more colorful, understanding of the religious landscape that shapes our world.

Read more at www.michaelpclutton.com.

# Also by Michael Clutton

**Hooked On Reel Fishing**
How to Tackle Saltwater Fishing
Big Game Fishing
Off Shore Fishing Adventures


**The Juice Chronicles**
Bloodlines: The Juice Chronicles


**Your Great Big Grab Bag of Useless Helpful Tidbits**
Charity Giving Donation Revelation
300 Trashy Truths You Didn't Need to Know


Watch for more at www.michaelpclutton.com.

# About the Author

Michael P. Clutton isn't your typical storyteller. Since he was young, he loved drawing cartoons and writing stories, which not only kept him busy but also helped him learn more words. This early passion for fiction laid the foundation for his unique voice—rich, imaginative, and brimming with wit.

Michael's sarcastic and unique perspective on life adds intrigue to his daily routine and captivates those around him. Known for his quick wit and self-deprecating humor, he can generate a giggle or a guffaw at the drop of a hat. His creative toolbox is well-stocked with both artwork and the written word, making him a versatile and dynamic creator.

Discover the captivating world of Michael P. Clutton, an author who combines humor, heart, and a deep passion for creativity in his stories and art.

Read more at www.michaelpclutton.com.